T0005170

# WANDERING ANIMALS

## Migration Stories from the Animal World

### Sharlene G. Coombs

**KNOWLEDGE BOOKS**

© Knowledge Books and Software

## Teacher Notes:

Animal migration is one of the great wonders of the natural world. For thousands of years, many different animals have come together in huge herds to journey over land, water, and across the skies. Their animal instinct helps them find their way to food, water, mating, and breeding grounds. Along the way, they keep their ecosystem healthy and strong and help sustain the balance it needs to survive.

### Discussion points for consideration:

1. Why do you think animals often migrate in large numbers? Discuss the term, "safety in numbers".

2. Discuss the problem with putting up fences along the wildebeest migration path. What other animals are impacted by this?

3. Why do we need to conserve these migrations? Discuss ecosystem balance and how these animals are part of the much larger food web.

### Difficult words to be introduced and practiced before reading this book:

migration, thousands, Antarctica, Southern, Australia, pregnant, calves, Pacific, protected, curious, Queensland, September, tourist, beautiful, wildebeest, antelope, Africa, Serengeti, annual, crocodile, predators, scavengers, pollution, challenges, researchers.

# Contents

1. What is Animal Migration?

2. Why do Animals Migrate?

3. When do Animals Migrate?

4. Humpback Whales

5. Wildebeest

6. Christmas Island Red Crab

7. Green Turtle

8. Migration Challenges

## 1. What is Animal Migration?

Animals are very clever! Some animals can survive with little food and water. If they run short of food or water, some animals even know where to find it.

Some animals even return to the place where they were born. This can be thousands of miles away. This is called animal migration.

Migration means to travel a long distance from one place to another. Some animals have been migrating for thousands of years. Why do you think they do this?

## 2. Why do Animals Migrate?

Animals migrate for different reasons. Often, it is to search for food or water. Sometimes they migrate to find a mate. Other animals migrate to a better climate.

Many different animal groups migrate. Often, they will migrate together in huge numbers. This can happen across land, across water, or in the sky.

## 3. When do Animals Migrate?

Animals migrate in time with the seasons. They can travel many miles across land. Some animals migrate across large oceans. Some birds migrate from one country to another. They can fly thousands of miles during their journey.

However, all animals that migrate have one thing in common. They all return back to where they came from. This can take weeks, months, or even years to happen.

## 4. Humpback Whales

Humpback whales are huge mammals. They eat krill and small fish. Krill look like tiny prawns or shrimp.

It takes a lot of krill to keep a humpback whale happy! This is why they spend their summer in the waters around Antarctica. The waters there are full of krill.

Once they have fattened up from their huge feed of krill, they will start their migration north. They leave the cold waters of the Southern Ocean in pods. They head together to the East Coast of Australia.

The water there is warmer. Many of the adult females are pregnant during this journey. This is another reason for their migration north. Humpback calves would not survive being born in the cold waters off Antarctica.

You can see humpback whales migrating along the East Coast of Australia from around June each year. It's a long journey for them.

Some of the females will start having their calves along the way. The calves are born in the warmer waters of the Pacific Ocean. They suckle from their mothers to grow stronger. They are also protected by the other whales in the pod.

Whale watching has become very popular along the East Coast of Australia. People love to watch whales as they migrate north.

The whales seem to like having the people around too! They can be very playful and curious. Some whales will swim right up to the boat and pop their head out of the water. It's like they are checking out the tourists! This is called spy-hopping.

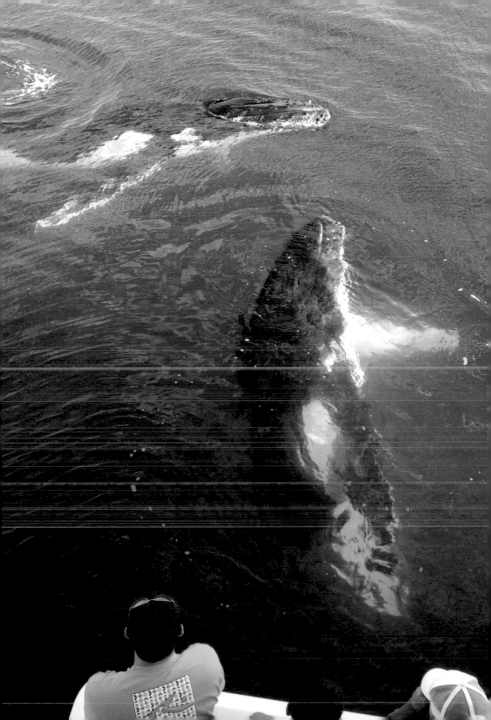

Humpback whales also love to jump right out of the water and come down with a big splash. This is called breaching.

Humpbacks migrate to the warmer waters off Queensland and rest there with their calves. Around September, they will start their migration back down the coast towards the Southern Ocean. All the calves have been born by this time. They are growing stronger and ready for their journey south.

The humpback whale migration is very important. If they did not migrate, they would not survive. Their migration has also become very important for tourists. Every year, many tourists love to watch these beautiful mammals on their journey.

## 5. Wildebeest

Wildebeest are a kind of antelope that live in Africa. They feed off grassy plains called the Serengeti. They can grow in huge numbers.

At the end of the rainy season, they start their annual migration north. They do this to search for better grasslands and water.

Wildebeest calves are born during the journey. It doesn't take them long before they are strong enough to keep up with the herd. Zebras can also join them along the way.

There are many dangers on the migration route. Wildebeest must cross rivers along the way. These rivers are also home to the Nile crocodile. Many wildebeest are taken by the crocodiles during these crossings. Others sometimes drown after being trampled on.

Predators like lions follow the wildebeest migration. They prey on the slower or younger animals that can't keep up with the herd.

This is no ordinary migration! Over 1.5 million wildebeest can migrate every year. Their migration looks like a huge loop around Africa. It can even be seen from space!

Some wildebeest will travel almost 1,000 miles in one year. It is the longest overland migration in the world.

23

## 6. Christmas Island Red Crab

The Christmas Island red crab lives on Christmas Island in the Indian Ocean. It is a land crab and lives in the rainforest. The young crabs live among the forest floor for the first 3 years of their life. They eat leaves, fruit, and small, dead animals. They are scavengers.

After the first 3 years of their life, they start migrating every year. They come together to make a huge migration to the coast. Why do you think they do this?

Red crabs leave their forest burrows at the beginning of the wet season. Their journey to the coast takes about a week.

During this time, much of the island is covered in red crabs. Imagine over 40 million crabs on the move! The local people must be careful not to run over them.

Once they get to the coast, the mating begins. The male crabs then return to the forest. The female crabs stay behind on the beach to lay their eggs. They have an egg pouch in their abdomen.

About 2 weeks later, they release their eggs into the ocean. They then return to the forest as well. About a month later, the baby crabs return to land. They find their way to the rainforest and join the others.

## 7. Green Turtle

The green turtle is one of the largest sea turtles in the ocean. It lives in the tropical waters of the Pacific Ocean.

Wherever there is seagrass, you can usually find green turtles. This is one of their favorite foods. It's also good for the seagrass to get a trim. Green turtles are like the lawnmowers of the sea!

The migration of the sea turtle is very special. Most turtles spend their whole life at sea. They migrate between feeding areas and places where they mate.

Females will only leave the ocean to lay their eggs. Every year, the female will migrate to the same place to lay her eggs. This is also the same spot where she was born. How cool is that!

After her long journey across the sea, the female green turtle arrives back to the same spot. She is very tired, but she still has a big job ahead of her.

She crawls slowly up the sand and chooses a spot, high up on the beach. She uses her flippers to dig a deep hole. Then she lays about 100 eggs which she covers with sand. She then slowly heads back out to sea again.

About 60 days later, the baby turtles hatch from their eggs together. They dig their way to the surface. This usually happens at night-time when there are less predators around.

It's then a rush to the water for all of them. They need to hurry because predators are waiting for them. Not all of them will make it to the water. Those that do get to the water need to swim fast to get to deeper water.

Only about 1 in 1000 hatchlings will make it to be adults. It's very risky being a baby turtle in the ocean!

## 8. Migration Challenges

Animals have been migrating for thousands of years. However, many things affect their journey. Humpback whales have been caught in shark nets when swimming too close to beaches. Some tourists don't follow the rules about giving them their space in the water.

Fences have been put up in many areas in Africa for cattle stations. However, they have also stopped the migration of the wildebeest in some areas. This stops them from getting to food and water and many are dying. If these animals die out, predators like lions and hyenas will also suffer.

Pollution is a very big problem for green turtles. They swallow plastic bags, thinking they are jellyfish. They get caught up in fishing nets and lines. Foxes and wild dogs sometimes dig up the eggs and eat them. Some of the nesting sites have been damaged or destroyed.

However, good things are also being done to help protect these animals. Humpback whales and sea turtles are now protected in many oceans. Many researchers are working with these animals to make life easier for them. This includes making sure that they can continue to migrate the way they have done for thousands of years.

# DO NOT DISTURB
# SEA TURTLE
# NEST

## VIOLATORS SUBJECT TO FINES AND IMPRISONMENT

**FLORIDA LAW CHAPTER 379.2431(1)**

No person may take, possess, disturb, mutilate, destroy, cause to be destroyed, sell, offer for sale, transfer, molest, or harass any marine turtle or its nest or eggs at any time.

Upon conviction, a person may be imprisoned for a period of up to 60 days or fined up to $500, or both, plus an additional penalty of $100 for each sea turtle egg destroyed or taken.

**U.S. ENDANGERED SPECIES ACT OF 1973**

No person may take, harass, harm, pursue, hunt, shoot, wound, kill, trap, or capture any marine turtle, turtle nest, and/or eggs, or attempt to engage in any such conduct.

Any person who knowingly violates any provision of this act may be assessed a civil penalty up to $25,000 or a criminal penalty up to $100,000 and up to one year imprisonment.

**SHOULD YOU WITNESS A VIOLATION, OBSERVE AN INJURED OR STRANDED TURTLE, OR MISORIENTED HATCHLINGS, PLEASE CONTACT FWC AT**

**1-888-404-FWCC** OR **✱FWC** **(MOBILE PHONE)**
FLORIDA FISH AND WILDLIFE CONSERVATION COMMISSION
MARINE TURTLE PROTECTION PROGRAM

P
73
CC
5.20

42

## Word Bank

migration

thousands

Antarctica

Southern

Australia

pregnant

calves

Pacific

protected

curious

Queensland

September

tourist

beautiful

wildebeest

antelope

Africa

Serengeti

annual

crocodile

predators

scavengers

pollution

challenges

researchers